PICTURE LIBRARY
SHIPS

N. S. Barrett

Franklin Watts

London   New York   Sydney   Toronto

© 1984 Franklin Watts Ltd

First published in Great Britain
  1984 by
Franklin Watts Ltd
12a Golden Square
London W1

First published in the USA by
Franklin Watts Inc
387 Park Avenue South
New York
N.Y. 10016

First published in Australia by
Franklin Watts
1 Campbell Street
Artarmon, NSW 2064

UK ISBN: 0 86313 197 2
US ISBN: 0-531-03722-3
Library of Congress Catalog Card
Number: 84-50699

Printed in Italy

Designed by
McNab Design

Photographs by
Australian News and Information Service
Ben Odeco Ltd
BP International
British Telecom
Cunard
Japan Ship Centre
The Mansell Collection
Novosti Press Agency
OCL
P&O Group
Port of Le Havre Authority
Princess Cruises
Prudential Lines
Shell Photo Service
Townsend Thoresen
Trinity House
Woods Hole
    Oceanographic Institute

Illustration by
P&O Group

Technical Consultant
Robert Shopland

Contents

Introduction

Every day, thousands of ships set out from ports all over the world. They carry passengers and cargo across seas and oceans. The largest ocean liners can carry more than 2,000 passengers. Most of these liners are used to take people on cruises. Smaller passenger ships carry people from place to place across seas and lakes.

△ An ocean liner lies anchored in a harbor. People on cruises visit resorts and other places of interest.

Ships can carry huge amounts of cargo. There are different types of cargo ships. Tankers have large tanks in their hulls for carrying liquids such as oil. Bulk carriers transport grain, coal and similar materials. Container ships carry their cargo in large oblong boxes. Some ships are used for special tasks such as laying cables.

△ Oil tankers are among the largest ships afloat. Compare their size with the two tugs on the right of the picture.

The liner

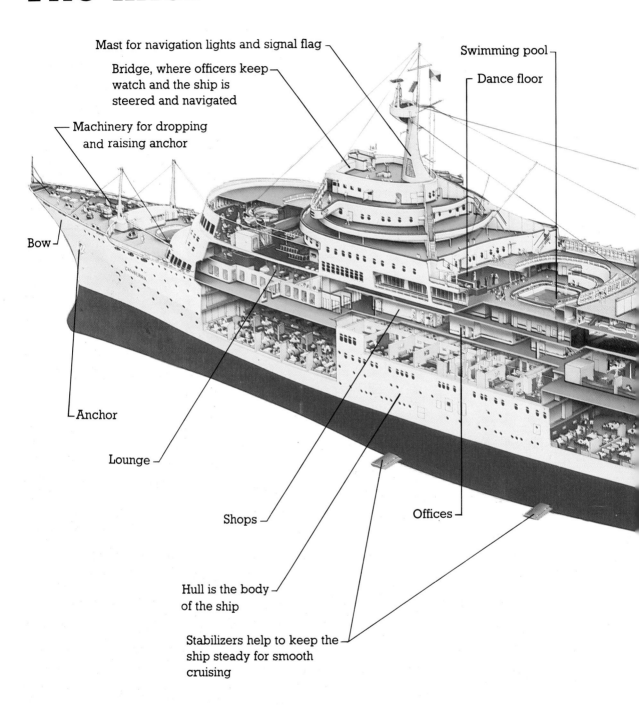

Mast for navigation lights and signal flag

Bridge, where officers keep watch and the ship is steered and navigated

Swimming pool

Dance floor

Machinery for dropping and raising anchor

Bow

Anchor

Lounge

Shops

Offices

Hull is the body of the ship

Stabilizers help to keep the ship steady for smooth cruising

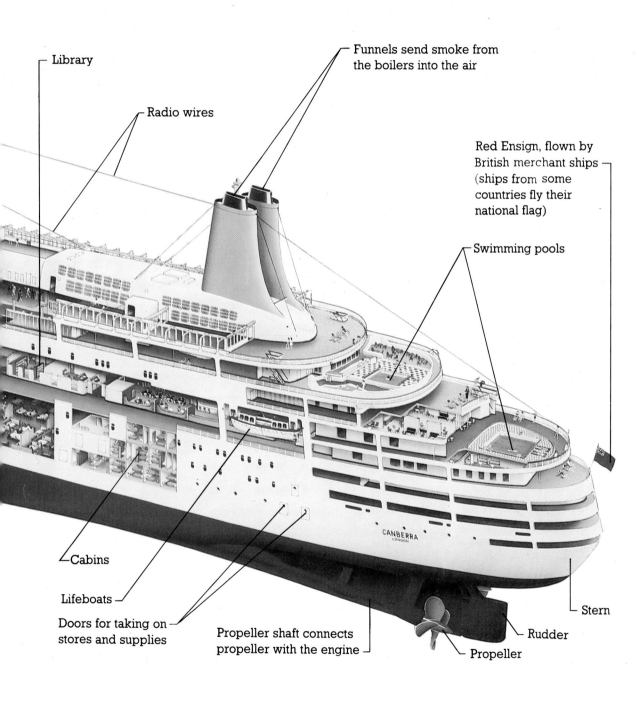

Library

Radio wires

Funnels send smoke from
the boilers into the air

Red Ensign, flown by
British merchant ships
(ships from some
countries fly their
national flag)

Swimming pools

Cabins

Lifeboats

Doors for taking on
stores and supplies

Propeller shaft connects
propeller with the engine

Propeller

Rudder

Stern

CANBERRA
LONDON

9

Ocean liners

Before people were able to travel by air, they used ships to cross the oceans. But a ship takes days for a journey that a jet airliner can do in hours. Today, most big ocean liners take people on pleasure cruises. They are like floating hotels. People sleep in comfortable cabins, and eat in large dining rooms. They can swim in pools or play games.

△ The *Queen Elizabeth 2* is one of the world's largest ocean liners. In the picture, fuel is being loaded.

△Passengers enjoy the sun on a cruise liner. There is also plenty to do inside. There are game rooms for people of all ages, and playrooms for young children.

◁A small cabin on a liner. This is an "outside" cabin, because it has a porthole (window) that looks out to sea.

Ocean liners take people to interesting places all over the world. The liners can visit islands or sail up large rivers or along coasts to big cities. Passengers can make shore trips when the liner reaches a port.

△ In some places, liners have to drop anchor away from the shore. Passengers may be taken ashore by motor boats.

▷ The cruise liner *Canberra*.

Ferries

Ferries are ships that take people on short trips across bodies of water. Some trips take less than an hour. Some ferries sail overnight and may have cabins for passengers to sleep in.

Many ferries take cars, trucks and buses. People leave their vehicles parked on the lower decks, and spend the trip on the upper decks.

△ A car ferry. Some ferries can carry as many as 300 cars and 1,000 passengers.

△A ferry captain works the controls to steer the ship out of harbor.

◁Motorists drive their cars on and off ferries.

Cargo ships

Big oil tankers are the largest ships in the world. They are called supertankers. The boiler room and engine room are at the stern of the ship. The officers and crew live and work above these. The rest of the ship contains huge oil tanks.

On some tankers, the deck is so long that the crew uses bicycles to get from one end to the other.

△ Tugboats push an oil tanker into position at a loading station.

△ A fire-fighting exercise on a tanker. Special foam must be used on ships carrying oil or chemicals.

◁ The captain of a tanker instructs cadets learning about the ship's controls.

Loading and unloading cargo on ships is a skilled job. Dockers spend a lot of time fitting cargo of all shapes and sizes into compartments called holds. They have to make sure that the cargo will not get damaged during the voyage. Today, special ships carry cargo packed into "containers." The containers are taken straight off trucks at the ports.

△ Containers are stacked on the deck as well as in the holds. Containers are made in standard sizes. They are 8 ft (2.44 m) high and wide. Most containers are 20 ft (6.10 m) or 40 ft (12.19 m) long.

There are other ways of loading cargo onto ships to save time and money. Barges called "lighters" can be floated straight on to a LASH vessel at anchor. Tugboats pull or push the lighters into position. LASH stands for Lighter Aboard SHip.

Another kind of cargo ship is like a huge car ferry. Trucks drive straight on with their loads and travel aboard the ship. This is called "roll-on, roll-off," or "Ro-Ro."

△ A tug pushes a lighter on board a LASH ship. Other lighters, all loaded with cargo, are at the side of the ship, waiting to be floated in.

19

Bulk carriers, which carry cargo such as grain or coal, are easy to load. Their cargo does not have to be packed or stacked. It can often be pumped or poured into the holds. The cargo fills every corner of the hold. Grain can be unloaded by machines that suck it out. Coal may be taken out by mechanical buckets.

△ A special loading bay for containers. Freight is packed into a container at the factory. The container is then loaded onto a flat truck, which takes it to the docks. A traveling crane lifts the container and stacks it in place on the ship.

△ This coal carrier has
nine hatches opening
onto separate holds.
Each hatch can carry a
different grade of coal.

◁ A product carrier has
separate tanks for
transporting many
different liquids. This
one has 33 tanks, all
with separate pipelines.

Special Ships

Many ships are built for special tasks. Icebreakers carve a way through the ice to clear a passage for other ships. Small tugboats, or tugs, help to move large ships in and out of harbors. They can tow or push big ocean liners or tankers.

Some ships are built for scientific work, such as studying the ocean or taking weather readings.

△ The Russian icebreaker *Lenin*. Icebreakers are used to keep frozen ports open in the winter months. They have very strong hulls, and ride up on the ice, crushing it with their weight. They clear a passage wide enough for the ships following them, and lead them into ice-free waters.

A lightship is a floating lighthouse. Lightships are anchored in places where lighthouses cannot be built. Their lights warn ships of danger.

Weather ships patrol areas of ocean. They have instruments that measure the wind, temperature and other weather conditions. Cable ships lay or repair telephone cables at the bottom of the ocean.

△ Lightships are anchored in position. The crew looks after the light and other equipment such as the radio beacon and fog signal.

△ The Russian ship *Vladimir Komarov* is one of the strangest looking vessels afloat. The two huge "balls" and the smaller one in between are radar domes. They can send and receive signals from great distances. The ship is used for scientific work connected with space-craft and satellites.

◁ A cable is laid from the bow of the ship. The bow of a cable ship is specially shaped for doing this.

△Research ships are used to study the oceans. They carry special instruments for taking measurements in the water and for studying sea life.

◁The crew of a research ship prepares to drop measuring equipment overboard.

Huge amounts of oil have been found under the seas in many parts of the world. Giant oil rigs are anchored out at sea to drill for this oil. Special ships are used to keep these rigs in working order and to deliver supplies. Some ships are used to drill for oil. Drill ships must be well anchored so that they remain still in rough seas.

△ A drill ship. The drilling is done through the bottom of the boat.

▷ Special ships are used to look after oil rigs. A service ship (above right) is used for repairs. A supply ship (right) takes equipment and materials.

The story of ships

Sail

People have sailed the seas for thousands of years. Sailing boats are powered only by the wind. At one time, sail was the only way to move ships. People still sail for pleasure in dinghies and yachts.

△ Once sailing ships ruled the seas.

Steam

The steam engine was invented in the early 1800s. The first ships powered by steam were built over 175 years ago. The steam engine worked a paddle-wheel, which drove the ship through the

△ A paddle steamer of 150 years ago.

water. The first steamboats also used sails. Even transatlantic liners kept sails in case of emergencies until about 100 years ago.

Propellers

Ships are now driven through the water by propellers. These work under the water. Their blades turn through the water in the same way as a screw turns through wood. For this reason, propellers are also called screws. The bigger ships have

△ A propeller-driven steamer of 1894.

more than one propeller. Propellers replaced paddle-wheels in the mid-1800s. Paddle-wheels worked well on rivers, but were often damaged in heavy seas.

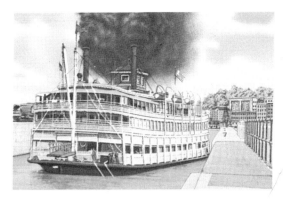

△ A river steamboat in the USA.

From wood to steel

Until about 150 years ago, ships were made of wood. Then shipbuilders began to use iron. It was stronger and safer than wood, and easier to repair. About 100 years ago, steel replaced iron. Aluminum is now used as well as steel. It makes the ship lighter.

From coal to oil

The steam for driving ships was produced by burning coal in furnaces. Gangs of men called "stokers" used to shovel the coal in. About 60 years ago, ships began to use oil for fuel. Oil-burning ships do not need stokers.

Giants of the ocean

Huge ships were built for carrying people across the oceans. The biggest of these was the *Queen Elizabeth*, finished in 1940. The longest ocean liner is the *Norway*, 1,035 ft (315 m) long. The biggest ships now are the supertankers. Some are nearly $1\frac{1}{2}$ times the length of the *Norway*.

△ A great liner, the *Queen Elizabeth*.

Back to sail

In 1980, a Japanese tanker called the *Shinaitoku Maru* was launched. It is a most unusual sight, because it has two sails. The sails are rigid, made of steel and canvas. They are worked by the push of a button. They make use of the wind and help to save fuel.

△ The *Shinaitoku Maru*, a "sailing" tanker.

Facts and records

The Blue Riband

Before the days of high-speed jet aircraft, the chief means of travel between Europe and the United States was by passenger liner. The shipping lines from different countries competed against each other to make the fastest crossing of the Atlantic Ocean. The fastest ship was said to hold the "Blue Riband" of the Atlantic. Ships from Britain, Germany, France, Italy and the United States won the Blue Riband at various times. At first there was no prize. But a silver trophy was

△ The British liner *Mauretania* of the Cunard Line first won the Blue Riband in 1907. She held it until 1929.

awarded in the 1930s. The last ship to win it was the *United States*, in 1952. This great American liner crossed the Atlantic in less than $3\frac{1}{2}$ days, a record that still stands.

△ The *Titanic* sinks, with a terrible loss of life.

The "unsinkable"

One of the most famous of all ocean liners never completed its first voyage. It was the *Titanic*, a British steamer and at the time the largest ship in the world. It was thought to be unsinkable. But, sailing from England to the United States in April, 1912, it hit an iceberg. Within $2\frac{1}{2}$ hours it had sunk. About 1,500 lives were lost.

The Queen Mary

The British liner *Queen Mary*, built in the mid-1930s, was a popular Atlantic passenger ship. She was used as a troopship in World War II. After the war, she again sailed the Atlantic, carrying nearly 2,000 passengers on each trip. In 1967, she was taken out of service. The *Queen Mary* now stands at Long Beach, California, and is used as a museum and hotel.

Glossary

Anchor
The anchor is a heavy weight used to hold a ship in place. Large ships might have two or more anchors. They are lowered and raised on the ends of heavy chains. Anchors are like giant metal hooks, and catch in the sand at the bottom of the water.

Bow
The front part of a ship.

Bridge
The platform above the main deck. Officers and crew on the bridge steer and navigate the ship.

Bulk carrier
A ship that carries cargo such as coal or grain. This type of cargo spreads out to fill the holds.

Container
A large box used for carrying cargo. Containers are made in standard sizes. They stack neatly on container ships.

Funnel
Funnels, or smokestacks, take smoke and fumes from the engines into the air. They are like exhaust pipes on cars or motorbikes.

Hold
The holds are the parts of the hull used for storing cargo.

Hull
The hull is the body of a ship. It is watertight (it does not let water in). The holds and the engine room are located inside the hull.

Lifeboat
A large ship carries many lifeboats. They can easily be lowered into the water in an emergency. There must be enough lifeboats to hold every person on board the ship.

Propeller
Propellers, or screws, are used to drive a ship. They are turned by the engines, through a shaft. Most ships have one or two propellers. Some have as many as four.

Rudder
The rudder is at the stern of a ship, below the water level. It is used to steer the ship. Some large ships have two rudders.

Stern
The back part of a ship.

Index